STEPPING STONES

*Wisdom to Encourage,
Inspire, and Comfort*

STEPPING STONES

*Wisdom to Encourage,
Inspire, and Comfort*

Pamela Crofoot Desvernine

Legacy Light Publishing
San Francisco, California

All inquiries should be directed to:
info@pameladesvernine.com
Legacy Light Publishing San Francisco, CA
info@legacylightbooks.com

Book Design and Production by Francis Fitzpatrick
Cover Art © 2020 by Francis Fitzpatrick
Interior Artwork Stonerose © 2020 by Francis Fitzpatrick
Author Photo of Pamela Crofoot Desvernine © 2015 by Dörthe Tatum
Photo of Graham "Des" Desvernine © 2018 by Carrie Thomsen
Content and Proof Editors: Francis Fitzpatrick and Georgia Coward
Content Readers: Freida Sparks, John I. Rigoli, Heather Olivier

Library of Congress Cataloging-in-Publication Data
Desvernine, Pamela Crofoot
      Stepping Stones: Wisdom to Encourage, Inspire, and Comfort/ Pamela Crofoot
Desvernine. —First edition.
Library of Congress Control Number: 2021908121
      Summary: In *Stepping Stones*, Pamela Crofoot Desvernine reveals and illustrates
how universal spiritual principles influence our lives and society. Through humor and
personal experiences, she weaves together ancient wisdom with practical skills to lift
self-esteem, improve interpersonal communications, harmonize relationships, and
promote a kinder, more inclusive world.
ISBN: 978-0-9978354-9-6 (pbk)
      1. Body, Mind Spirit-Inspiration & Personal Growth 2. Self-Help/ Self-Esteem
3. Relationships/ Communication 4. Social Issues/ Tolerance 5. Interfaith / Spirituality

This Book is Dedicated with Heartfelt Love and Gratitude
to...

My Beloved Husband
Graham "Des" Desvernine

and...

My Wonderful Family
On Both Sides of the Veil

ACKNOWLEDGEMENTS

It is a pleasure to acknowledge and thank many of those who provided the stepping stones of spiritual teachings along my path. I have been especially influenced and blessed by the writings and teachings of Dr. Ernest Holmes, Dr. William H.D. Hornaday, Rev. Dr. Margaret Stortz, Rev. Dr. Terry Cole-Whittaker, Rev. Florence Becker, Rev. Louise Irvine, Rev. Dr. Kathy Hearn, Rev. Dr. Don Mc Art, Louise L. Hay, and Rev. Wilma Arnott.

From conception to manifestation, my beloved and talented goddaughter Francis Fitzpatrick, has contributed unwavering vision, editing skills, technical expertise, and loving support to this project. It would not have happened without her.

Thanks also to my beautiful mother Vicki, who embodied Divine Love, resourcefulness, creativity, and spiritual strength. My amazing sister and forever-friend Debra, blesses me daily with her understanding, laughter, spiritual compass, and love.

Special thanks also to the Prager-Flynns and the Morgans for their life-long friendship, encouragement, and for providing restorative sanctuaries.

This book was completed during the pandemic of 2020. I'm so grateful for the kindness of dear neighbors and friends who helped us function and cope during the quarantine. Thanks also to countless essential workers everywhere who helped us all through this historic challenge.

No words can express my gratitude to my Spirit Team for their guidance and constant proof of the continuity of life and love.

And finally, thanks to my beloved *Mr. Wonderful,* Graham *Des* Desvernine. His unconditional love has always inspired me to do my best and fulfill my divine potential. Our journey together for over 40 years was filled with laughter, adventures, service, and indefinable love. That journey, that love, continues today, transcending physical death. I have daily proof that there is no time or distance in love, and that life continues in the glorious *Realms of Light.*

CONTENTS

INTRODUCTION

*"Blessings happen when a heart opens
and we find all of us there within it."*
—David Spangler

The timeless truths I share in *Stepping Stones* formed the spiritual foundation of my life. The seeds of desire to compile them into a useful form have incubated in my heart for years. Desire and intention finally manifested— those seeds have fully flowered into this book. I have opened my heart, dear reader, and now *you* are my blessing.

The epic times we live in call for a balanced perspective, spiritual strength and practical action. It's apparent that today's concerns, challenges, and circumstances are extraordinary and may feel overwhelming. Yet in a bigger picture, the issues we face contain echoes of the past. Humanity has survived many previous pandemics, conflicts, and periods of climate change in our long planetary history. As individuals, we long for relief of anxiety and seek ways to help us handle our personal challenges and public concerns.

Is there somewhere to turn, something we can access to help us cope, hold steady, gain perspective, and navigate our daily lives? Is it possible to live with more clarity, harmony, and even joy irrespective of circumstances? I believe the answer is a resounding *Yes!* Help comes from the wisdom found in many cultures, the use of tried-and-true spiritual practices, and an understanding of the operating principles of Life. The essence and foundation of those principles is Love. We each have within us the potential to cultivate and use innate qualities and helpful techniques to live more peaceful, joyful, balanced, and loving lives.

Stepping Stones is a distillation of the golden threads of Truth found in Western, Eastern, and Metaphysical philosophies and religions. All of these traditions informed my ecumenical approach to spirituality. Each chapter provides effective techniques, affirmations, and practices for spiritual support.

The ideas shared here fortified my personal and professional path. In 1973, I became one of the first female managers of fine-dining restaurants at a time when women were rarely promoted to top management. Then, after marrying my husband Des, I gave support to him during his dangerous undercover roles with the F.B.I.

Most wives awaken to hear something like, "Coffee Honey?" Instead, I heard, "Honey I have a *meet* with the *wise guys* today. Could you get out that black silk shirt and patent shoes? My informant's bringing the gold chains and diamond horseshoe ring." During those years it was vital to maintain my faith, and surrender any fear about Des' safety. Upon his retirement from the F.B.I., Des formed a private investigations firm. I joined the company, managing the business for the next three decades. We handled cases ranging from international counterfeit operations to finding missing children. Every day we felt privileged to do meaningful work and help many people. By using the principles offered here, and putting Love to practical use, we were equipped to be effective with our clients. We also provided comfort to them as needed, and maintained our own positive perspective, emotional balance and spiritual strength.

I am eager to share with you the relevant and reliable wisdom, guidance, and spiritual tools that give me strength, poise, peace, and joy each day, *regardless* of ever-changing personal and world conditions. It is my sincere desire that the experiences and various practices offered here become *stepping stones* to encourage, inspire, and provide comfort along your own spiritual journey.

With Blessings, Joy, Love, and Gratitude,

Pamela Crofoot Desvernine

San Francisco, California

March 2021

A NOTE ABOUT
UNIVERSAL PRINCIPLES

The term *Universal Principles* is used several times in Stepping Stones. It is beyond the scope of this book to fully describe and illustrate these Principles; however, I'd like to share a few thoughts about them.

The word *universal* refers to an essence, quality, or pattern existing everywhere. A *Universal Principle* is a concept that is generally recognized by everyone as true. It is self-evident and observable regardless of one's understanding or belief in it.

We can observe the Universal Principles of Divine Intelligence and Order operating in Nature. For instance, we witness the symbiotic relationships between insects and plants to facilitate pollination. We marvel at the exquisite design and function of a beehive, or the mystery of how caterpillars emerge as butterflies from cocoons. Miraculously, we can be certain that a natural tomato seed will always produce tomatoes and never corn or zucchini. On the invisible plane we know gravity exists even though we cannot see it—just its effects.

Likewise, Universal Spiritual Principles operate on the invisible plane, primarily experienced as cause and effect. For example, what we Love will generally flourish, what we praise will likely improve, what we water physically and metaphorically will grow.

This book endeavors to reveal how the conscious application of the Universal Spiritual Principle of Love will enhance and improve all areas of our lives.

A BAG OF TOOLS

Isn't it strange that Princes and Kings,
And Clowns that caper in sawdust rings,
And common folk like you and me
Are builders of Eternity?

To each is given a bag of tools,
A shapeless mass, and a Book of Rules;
And each must make, e'er time has flown,
A stumbling block, or a stepping stone.

—R.L. Sharpe 1809

THE DIVINE BLUEPRINT

The most beautiful and enduring earthly structures are first conceived in imagination. Then, a skilled architect makes a detailed blueprint from which the builder manifests the vision. God is the Creator and Divine Architect of our being. We are each a unique and Holy Temple consisting of mind, body, soul, and spirit. We come into physical incarnation from God's Blueprint of spiritual perfection, conceived in Divine Love. The Divine Blueprint carries our spiritual DNA, the eternal Divine spark of life, and all the qualities of the Great Creator. Your Divine Blueprint is given with the gift of life itself; you do not have to earn it. As an individualized expression of God, your soul is the bridge between your physical body and spiritual nature. The soul grows through human experience. Our lives well lived, become a prayer of gratitude to the Creator.

In our own lives, we are the builders authorized to modify and manifest the Divine Blueprint, revealing the full potential of our own Holy Temple. Amazingly, the Divine Architect has given us imagination and free will to alter and even make design changes to the original plan. To be successful, we must learn the mental, spiritual and physical laws of the Universe. These become our firm foundation to withstand the challenges of health, relationships, finances, and shifting world conditions.

There is a Masonic parable that tells of three masons who were laying bricks. A man walked up to them and asked each one the same question:

What are you doing?

The first mason spit on the ground, looked up and said,

"I'm laying bricks. What does it look like I'm doing?"

The second mason mopped his brow and groaned,

"I'm earning a living."

The third mason looked up with light in his eyes and said,

"I'm building a Cathedral."

The brick masons show us that motive and anticipation of good outcomes are powerful. It has often been said that energy flows where attention goes. It is important to understand that the energy of physical matter actually coalesces around thoughts. This is the Law of Mind in which thoughts become form and experience.

I believe that many of us are here trying to do our best to build a good life for ourselves and others, making this world a better place. We have the power to create, change, and improve the results of any situation with our conscious and consistent thoughts. The Divine Blueprint is animated by Divine Unconditional Love. Understand that you are an inseparable beam of light radiating from the Source at all times. You are a cherished and unique expression of God. Your Divine Blueprint has unlimited potential.

The truth is that we are completely connected to *All Life in the Oneness of God*. Separation is an illusion. We can view and experience the world as a more friendly and cooperative place by knowing that *All is One*; and that we are a necessary and beloved part of the Whole. Once you realize that the qualities of God express *as* and *through* you, feelings of inadequacy, despair, or hopelessness lose their power. When we identify ourselves truly as an expression of God, life becomes simpler, easier, and more harmonious. We realize that we have the power, intelligence and love of God within us to meet any challenge or circumstance. What we perceive as challenges, mistakes, or injuries become part of the whole experience on the continuum of our spiritual development. We build our trust and faith in God's Divine plan and realize there is a bigger picture than we now perceive.

Helping or uplifting another brings blessings to both the giver and receiver. It affirms our connectedness with each other. One of my beloved teachers, the Rev. Dr. Margaret Stortz once said, "Service is love in work clothes." If we are making a decision, she suggests that we ask ourselves: *Does what I am about to say or do build up or tear down myself or others?* Love always affirms and enhances life. Sometimes speaking our truth is difficult for others to hear. Let us be sensitive and maintain a compassionate tone. Change may be difficult and slow; yet we must be patient. We do not have to lose our own peace and equilibrium in manifesting necessary changes.

You are the Holy Temple. Wherever you stand is

Holy Ground. There is a never-ending supply of new materials and opportunities to grow at the temple site. Kahlil Gibran says it simply, "Your daily life is your temple and your religion." Embrace the power of persistent daily practices: prayer, healthy habits, and positive attitudes. Also remember, you are worthy of your own kindness, care, and encouragement! You are fulfilling your Divine Purpose every day as a sanctuary of love and light, and as a distribution center of compassion and service.

Thought-by-thought we build and maintain our Holy Temple of body, mind, and soul. Our spiritual blueprint is conceived in the perfection of God's Mind. Through free will, we make modifications by activating our imagination and making choices. The Divine Blueprint gives us guidelines for a firm foundation and unlimited potential for our temple. Through meditation and introspection, we recognize that we are the beloved of God. Let us refer often to our Divine Blueprint of love and endeavor to bring it to glorious manifestation as God intended for our highest good and greatest joy.

AFFIRMATIONS
I build on the firm foundation of God's Divine Plan for me.
I co-create my life using my unique Divine Blueprint.

I continue to grow and fulfill my Divine Purpose with Love.

OUR SPIRITUAL TOOL KIT

O ur life on Earth provides the opportunity to reveal the Divine Blueprint that Creator God has given each one of us, and to co-create the living temple of our lives. We can ask ourselves: *Do I see myself as a beautiful Holy Temple of God? How do I build, renovate, or modify my temple? What materials and tools can I use?*

In 1971, my dear friend Barbara Prager gave me the *Diligent Duchess* tool kit when I moved into my first nice apartment. All the tools had handles made of clear Lucite with silver glitter embedded in them—I love and still use them! I started thinking about how we could use common tools to remind us of the spiritual thoughts and principles that help us build our lives more effectively. As the builder and caretaker of your Holy Temple, what can you access to build, repair, support, reinforce and improve it? *What's in your Spiritual Tool Kit?*

A **Hammer** is most effective when used with power and repetition. We can apply that idea to using affirmations. They become more effective spiritual tools when used consistently and repeatedly. Create affirmations that are powerful and meaningful. Recite them often. The following are a few affirmations of truth to hammer into your subconscious mind:

I am a Beloved Child of God, and Divine Love is my Essence.

My good comes from the substance of Spirit; I use my thoughts to strengthen my conscious connection with Spirit.

Everything I need to build a healthy and happy life is within me.

We gain most of our spiritual growth during times of challenge and crisis. It rarely develops when we're on vacation or when life is going easy. We summon our spiritual strength with affirmations. Our prayers and practices become important in our spiritual tool kit. We diligently cultivate and activate spiritual strength and authority through the repetition and persistence of the **Hammer**, so keep it handy.

Pliers help us to *get and keep a grip* on our thoughts

and emotions. We can pull out the *rusty nails* of obsolete beliefs and attitudes. Let us keep a secure hold on life-affirming thoughts and habits.

The **Adjustable Wrench** reminds us to adapt to circumstances. This tool can be modified and applied for different purposes. Similarly, as we build our repertoire of prayers and practices, we can apply the most helpful tool for each situation that may arise. Remember, it's not *what* happens, it's *how* we deal with it that determines our inner soul's growth. We have the power to change our thought about anything. *Whatever comes up, I can handle it.*

Let's use the **Measuring Tape** as a symbol for evaluating progress. It's important to measure our spiritual growth. As you grow, acknowledge how much more patient, kind and loving you are to yourself and others. Notice when you are more compassionate and tolerant. Appreciate when you take more personal responsibility for your thoughts and the life you are building. Look at yourself through the eyes of patience and compassion. Always do your best, praising your efforts and service, even if the results are less than perfect. When we do our best in any given moment, we avoid judgment and regrets. My friend Blanche

Yarbrough always said, "I do my best, and let God do the rest." Remember to give thanks for your progress each day.

A **Drafting Compass** symbolizes our ability to set boundaries. As we know, a compass has two prongs; one with a sharp point which anchors the tool to the paper, and one that holds a pencil to draw circles of varying radiuses around the center point. This tool illustrates how we can draw physical, mental, emotional, and spiritual boundaries at various distances around the core of our being.

We have the choice and responsibility to set boundaries in all areas of our lives. There's a wide range of intimacy levels in our relationships. Our primary connection to Source is anchored in our souls, our center point. Extending from our core, the circles of intimacy expand outward, to family, friends and colleagues, and on to acquaintances and humanity.

It takes healthy self-esteem and discernment to set and maintain your boundaries. Many of us have experienced unhealthy relationships. Practice setting strong boundaries by saying *No!* or *Enough!* to people who disrespect you or to situations that are harmful to you in any way. A healthy ego can protect you. Do not allow yourself to be a doormat! Monitor your physical, mental, emotional, and spiritual borders, opening them only when you see fit to do so. You are forever connected to a Loving God who cherishes you. Stay centered and love yourself.

A **Level** will help us stay emotionally, mentally, and physically balanced. Andrew Jackson Davis, one of the founders of Modern Spiritualism, gave us *The Magic Staff*, "In all circumstances, keep an even mind." Love is the great leveler, and keeps us in balance with ourselves and others. Filter all your thoughts, words, and actions through love, compassion, and tolerance. It's up to us to remember that we are all connected in the *One Eternal Life*. Each of us is a unique and necessary part of the Whole. Many people have forgotten who they really are as a spiritual being. They may have sunk into negativity and despair, or are behaving badly. Don't jump to conclusions based on appearances. Jerry Jampolsky reminds us to, "Look past their lampshade to their light." Practice putting a positive spin on things. If *you* don't shine your light and remain balanced, peaceful, and loving—*who will*?

Pruning Shears symbolize our power to cut out negativity, such as the destructive habits of complaining,

11

fear, and worry. We can also cut off the dead branches of old attitudes, judgments and criticisms. Prune off outworn thoughts and negative habits. Careful and conscious pruning facilitates healthy new growth.

Celebrating myself through personal flare, creative style, and self-expression gives me a lift and makes me smile. Landscaping my personal temple also includes a little *bling*. Choosing fun accessories is for me like decorating a garden with colorful plants and lights. We need not fear making positive changes which will help us flourish. Anäis Nin expressed it this way, "And the day came when the risk to remain closed tight in a bud became more painful than the risk it took to blossom."

Many spiritual practices and exercises are available; most people have used and mastered several. Choose your favorites; they all work—but *consistent daily practice* is the key to developing our spiritual strength and balance. A prayer, chant, mantra, music, or movement draws the focus to God, to your heart, to your spiritual center. There's an old story of a young musician visiting New York City who asked a local man how to get to the famous Carnegie Concert Hall. The old man answered, "Practice, practice, practice!" The Masters say to us, *We would be pleased if you would use even 10% of what you know!* Practice, practice, practice your *Practice!*

AFFIRMATIONS

I use my spiritual tools daily to stay Balanced, Confident, and Positive.

I have the courage to release old patterns and behaviors.

I have everything I need to build and maintain my Holy Temple.

GOD'S AMBASSADOR-AT-LARGE

Many years ago, I left a long-time position as a restaurant manager just before the holiday season. I decided to enjoy the holidays, and wait until the New Year to seek another job. I didn't realize, however, how dependent I had become on my business card, giving my position and contact information. Now that I was without a title, *who was I?* I actually struggled with my sense of identity, until I had a bigger thought. After meditating on my true identity as God's beloved, I gave myself a new title: *God's Ambassador-At-Large!*

I grew up with Gospel and traditional Christian music. One of my favorite songs is, *"This world is not my home, I'm just a-passin' through..."*. Sometimes we feel like a stranger in a strange land. Let's remember, we are on a temporary assignment, with an extended visit on

Earth. I believe our true and eternal home is Heaven, or as we often say, the Spirit World.

From ancient times to the present, in almost every world religion, we have descriptions and recorded accounts from those who have had glimpses of the Spirit World. Some people report seeing spirits, many have had near-death experiences that include glimpses of Heaven or visits with pre-deceased loved ones. The vast majority of descriptions include seeing a beautiful light and a feeling of love that cannot be adequately explained in words. I believe that we come from the heavenly realms to incarnate many times on Earth. Our souls evolve from these cycles—growing, learning, and serving. I believe our ultimate goal is to *become* and *reflect* the qualities of God, the Great Spirit of Life. I also believe that our souls come into the physical body and world with a divine assignment and unique purpose. We are given the opportunity to express, and purify ourselves and our thinking. We use our strengths, strengthen our weaknesses, developing our unique talents and gifts in service to God and the beings of Earth—our *temporary* residence.

What does it mean to be God's Ambassador-At-Large?

In our world culture, an Ambassador is expected to represent his or her country in the best, most gracious manner. They are also expected to build bridges of understanding and cooperation. Appreciating the differences in culture and attitudes promotes harmonious relations. As God's Ambassadors we employ these same standards, representing and sharing the spiritual qualities of Heaven in our daily lives on Earth.

What are the Qualities of God and Heaven that we want to embody and share?

In my neighborhood there is a beautiful Christian Science Church, built in 1913. Carved over each of the four entrance doors are these phrases: *God is Life; God is Truth; God is Light; God is Love.* What a great reminder for the hundreds of people who walk by each week! Additional qualities of God we can aspire to represent are: order, wisdom, joy, beauty, and harmony. All of these qualities have a special rate of vibration or aura, which is seen as light and color. In Heaven we are recognized by the light and colors we radiate, which are indicators of our thoughts and soul. Even in the dense atmosphere of Earth, we sense a person's energy and spirit, and many people do see auras of light and color around others.

In Matthew 5.14-16, Christ Jesus told the people: "You are the light of the world...let your light shine before all, that they may see your good deeds and praise your Father in Heaven." This is a clear description of our duty as Ambassadors for God and Heaven. We must use our unique qualities to serve the world, to shine our light, and to do good deeds. This is not for our own glory, but to praise the One we represent.

What are good deeds?

All good deeds are motivated by love and the Golden Rule: *Do unto others as you would have them do unto you.* Every major world religion has some version of this idea. The Dalai Lama puts it very simply: *Be Kind.* Love and kindness have a ripple effect, and even radiate from generation to generation. They affect our attitude and motive, which then translates into action and compassion. Hugh and Gayle Prather write in their book, Notes to Each Other, "The time will come when it will be unthinkable to take a break from kindness". Let us aspire to apply the Golden Rule to all our tasks, communications, and relationships.

As God's Ambassadors, we have unlimited territory and we are on duty everywhere we go. We must make our divine nature the core of our inner authority. We answer to God for our actions. It is suggested that we connect each day with our Heavenly Headquarters. Ask the Great Spirit these simple questions:

What would you have me know?

What would you have me say?

What would you have me do?

What is my Divine assignment today?

In order to maintain our balance and perspective in the midst of instability and prevalent fears, we must mindfully cultivate inner peace. Consciously get centered and tune to your inner guidance by any means you choose. You will then be prepared to meet situations with confidence, poise, and peace. To bring Heaven to Earth requires commitment, time, and inner discipline. We are charged with the high responsibility to represent the realms of Heaven. We condition ourselves through prayer, meditation, study, and practice. To be effective, we must learn all we can about Heaven, about our ultimate authority—God, and about the Universal Principles. We teach by example. God is counting on *us* to be kind, patient, helpful, and loving in all our relationships and activities. We build bridges, not walls as we exercise compassion in our daily lives.

The poem "Outwitted" by Edwin Markham illustrates

diplomacy and compassion at a very high level:

> *He drew a circle that shut me out-*
> *Heretic, rebel, a thing to flout.*
> *But Love and I had the wit to win:*
> *We drew a circle that took him in!*

Each of us has a Heavenly passport—it is LOVE; it will get us into every social circle and every positive relationship; it will get us past barriers of fear, judgment and social exclusion. Love can heal every human condition.

We are spiritual beings having a human experience. I believe we come from and go back to our Heavenly home. We are using this earthly experience to develop our understanding of the Universal Principles, and to give loving service. Upon our return to Heaven, we can expect to hear God say, *Well done, my good and faithful servant!*

AFFIRMATIONS
I am God's Ambassador-At-Large.
I am the Face, the Hands, and the Heart of God on Earth.
I am on a Divine Assignment to Love and serve today.

BRINGING HEAVEN TO EARTH

There is great interest about the intense cosmic, spiritual, and material changes on our planet. Numerous articles, books, and channelings stress the importance of staying connected to our inner guidance. By doing our daily practices, we stay balanced and positive in our mental attitudes. When we stay aware, stable, and positive we become the lighthouse for others. We bring the light of Heaven to Earth to help all humanity survive and thrive.

Change, whether we deem it positive or unwelcomed, can be difficult and even painful. On the material plane, sorting through old clothes, papers, and sentimental objects requires mental focus, intention, and a willingness to let go. The same is true spiritually. We must release old attitudes, thinking, and habits in order to make room for increasing good in our lives. It's not always easy or pleasant leaving behind what was familiar or comfortable in the past. Often this process can leave us feeling physically and emotionally overwhelmed, insecure, tired, perhaps even depressed. There may be energies or circumstances involved over which we may not have control.

But I have good news—there is real and symbolic light at the end of this tunnel! In fact, you don't have to wait until you reach the end! There's light and power within *you* right *now* that you can access and use. You are a divine spiritual being of light, and can turn within to your center of love and power for all the strength, wisdom, peace, and guidance you need at any moment, under any conditions. It is always important to cultivate the spiritual skills and resources to stay balanced.

More than ever before, it is important to have faith in the Universal Laws, to recognize that appearances and conditions around us are temporary, and to remember that our own thinking, choices, and actions make a positive difference. An affirmation I use often to help lift me out of the fear which is so prevalent in our world is: *God is turning everything to Good!*

As we observe the world, we see many familiar

systems and structures collapsing in governments and commerce. Additionally, humanity is negatively impacting Mother Earth and the elements. Powerful forces of Nature such as fire, water, and air are destabilized, resulting in extreme weather. This devastates populations of people, animals and plants. The South Atlantic Anomaly provides scientific evidence that even the magnetic field of our planet is weakening. Many of these changes are the consequences of human activity; other changes may be natural cycles. Regardless of cause, we must take urgent action to respect, protect and balance our relationship with Mother Nature.

Perhaps you have had personal circumstances that have been devastating to you, causing loss, grief, despair, or fear. Where can a person go to find guidance, comfort, healing, or a sense of strength and security? For me, it is in the quietness of my soul, the center of my heart. We tune in to that place through prayer and meditation. In the inner stillness, we hear the voice of love, hope and peace. Through daily practice, we build up a reserve of faith and strength to meet sudden changes, or to stay strong and balanced through prolonged challenges or troubled times.

I believe light dispels darkness of any kind, and that

Love is the most powerful element and energy in the Universe. I believe that love has the power to heal all conditions and circumstances, and that love is being revealed on this planet, and in all beings when they are born. I have no doubt that we are part of the team of light which is building the bridge into the *Golden Age of Love and Peace*. And it is happening each and every day— through you and me. We are bringing Heaven to Earth here and now!

Let's look at some of the heavenly qualities we can express in our earthly lives: seeing God in all; maintaining awareness of the unity of life; having faith in God's good; and bringing love to all encounters and communications. If you find yourself being less than heavenly, judging and criticizing others, or feeling fear, take those thoughts and move them from your head to your *heart.* Speak love, peace, and healing to yourself, to others, and to Mother Earth herself.

The following affirmations are a quick way to remind ourselves of the truth, and to bring us to our center of balance and peace:

The Power of Love is turning this experience to good.

With God there's always a way, always an answer.

God in me is coming through as wisdom and strength.

The *Light Invocation* is a favorite, powerful prayer created by scientist and crystal healer DaEl Walker. This prayer said in conjunction with the application of a quartz crystal to an area of body discomfort, reduced pain in test subjects. These studies were conducted at the University of California Pain Management Center in Los Angeles. The prayer also increases a person's light field as seen through a bio-photon camera. It is best repeated in cycles of three:

I invoke the light of God within.

I am a clear and perfect channel.

Light is my guide.

Another prayer I use often is the Buddhist *Metta*:

May I be at peace.

May my heart remain open.

May I awaken to the light of my own true nature.

May I be healed.

May I be a channel of healing for all beings.

When each of us makes our own candle brighter, we contribute to the collective light, and become agents of positive change. I believe the heavenly beings of light can work *with* us and *through* us to uplift this world, and everyone here. When we see everyone as our *Family-in-God*, we feel the unity of life, and we bring Heaven to Earth.

It's not easy to watch people who are being violent or spreading destruction and misery. How do we extend love to them? Spirit writings tell us that in Heaven they are looked upon with patience and compassion, because they have either forgotten, or never knew, that they are a child of God. They are seen as infants on the path of spiritual growth and awareness. Regardless of your opinion of people who do harmful, violent, or horrific acts, nothing but good will come if we continue to send prayers for their enlightenment, and send healing love, often from a safe distance. Doing this does *not* imply acceptance or approval of harmful, destructive, or violent actions. We go past their behavior, sending healing and light to their soul. As love and light grow and prevail on Earth, it will become unthinkable to do harm to another.

There are major cosmic and global changes happening. Personally, many of us are experiencing our own major challenges. It has often been said that, *The only way out is the way through*. We must stay connected to our Source of light and divine wisdom to navigate through these personal and global changes in order to emerge free, joyful, and healed.

The Spiritual Masters tell us that this evolution towards greater light is a *collective process*. We make personal progress when we heal our own attitudes of prejudice, negativity, and fear. This contributes to the spiritual progress of *all*. As my Mom used to say, "When one boat in the harbor is lifted they are all lifted." The light of love you shine each day makes a positive difference. You bring Heaven to Earth with each kindness, each smile, and each word of gratitude, praise and encouragement. Your faith and prayers are building the bridge between Heaven and Earth. Stay steady, stay connected to the *Source of Light and Love*, and *Keep Shining!*

AFFIRMATIONS
My true nature is Love.
I breathe in Light; I breathe out Love.
My Love brings Heaven to Earth today.

THE POWER OF YOUR WORDS

Words are an incredibly powerful form of energy, carried on our breath of life. Words communicate our thoughts and emotions whether they are spoken or written. We can deliberately alter how we feel by the words we choose.

Rev. Florence Becker in the <u>Science of Being</u> has a lot to say about what we give our breath of life to, reminding us that our spoken word has great power. She states, "Anything that's going out of you is coming back to you—so watch your tongue"! Furthermore, Rev. Becker asserts, "The spoken word is much more forceful than a thought. The spoken word is the Living Flame of God." Remember, "In the beginning was the Word..." John 1.1. The word precedes manifestation of the physical form.

There is intriguing research being done regarding the

effects of spoken words and sound vibrations upon the water molecule. Water contains electrical, magnetic, and chemical properties, and it even holds memory! Water is a superconductor, a recording medium of everything, including emotions. The information coming from water research is important to us, because our bodies are approximately 70% water.

John Stuart Reid, a sound engineer, has been doing some groundbreaking studies in *Cymatics*—making photographs of specific sound patterns. He has developed a device which provides a visual image of a person's unique voice pattern. This technology is currently being studied to detect diseases. There are also several studies documenting the use of specific sound frequencies to reduce inflammation in the body. Furthermore, there are new emerging technologies that use specially paired resonant frequencies to dissolve some types of cancerous tumors.

Our bodies react instantly to jarring sounds, or angry words becoming tense, agitated and upset. Conversely, our bodies relax and feel soothed with the beautiful sounds of nature, good music, or kind and encouraging words. The positive energies we direct to ourselves bring the water in our bodies into balance and harmony. When we project words of praise and gratitude to others and our environment, everything thrives.

For centuries, indigenous shamans, priests and healers have focused prayers, chants, mantras and sounds into water, charging it with healing intentions and making it *holy.* There are countless testimonies of the healing results. We have the power to create *holy water* within our own bodies with the use of healing words and loving intentions.

Let's look at words that Steal, words that Heal, and words that Reveal.

Words that *Steal*

The 8th Commandment given to Moses by God is, "You shall not Steal." We may be able to say that we've never taken something that didn't belong to us. But we may have to consider that it's likely we've all stolen from another with our words. When we say something unkind or critical to another, we are stealing their self-esteem and self-worth. When we interrupt someone telling a joke and steal their punch line, we take away their joy of sharing humor. When we break another's confidence in us, we steal their trust. Gossip is another very destructive form of stealing. Unkind or untrue words steal a person's good name, credibility, and reputation. We're seeing the extreme results of this in the tragedy of children taking their own lives because of gossip and bullying. If we are honest with ourselves, we may have to admit we have stolen from others by using unkind words.

In the March, 2011, issue of *Creative Thought* magazine, Rev. Sally Robbins tells of a teacher who challenged her class with the following assignment, "For the next week, don't say anything unkind, untrue, or unnecessary." No one made it through even one day, much less a week! This is an excellent challenge for ourselves to pay more attention to what we are saying—is it unkind, untrue, or unnecessary?

The use of words that harm or tear down *ourselves*, and steal our own self-confidence, are equally devastating. Phrases like, *I'm so stupid*, or *I can't do anything right*, or *I always mess things up*, are self-deprecating and negative. Harsh, mean, and unkind words make our souls wither and shrivel up.

It is extremely important to catch ourselves, and quickly delete negative, ugly, harmful or untrue things we say to or about ourselves. Replace them immediately and consciously with positive affirmations such as:

I may have goofed up, but I'm not stupid!

I am making better choices and decisions every day.

Spirit within me knows what to do and how to do it.

Replace the negative thoughts with the truth. If you cannot say something good or true to yourself or another, *keep silent*! Don't give your breath of life to the negative. Speak only life-affirming words that facilitate your desired feelings and experiences.

<u>Words that *Heal*</u>

For years I had a simple sign on my desk which read, *Be Kind.* This is a way we put love into action. Kind words heal, soothe, and uplift. Words of praise nourish everything from plants and animals, to the human soul. All of us can probably remember a time when the kind and validating words of someone gave us the courage to carry on, or try harder. Perhaps someone's praise even helped us change the way we value ourselves. The following are some examples of encouraging and kind words to say to yourself and others:

I love myself.

I am able and capable.

I made an excellent effort.

I appreciate you.

I'm proud of you!

I love you.

Words of compassion, kindness, encouragement,

and praise have an extraordinary capacity to change people and situations for the better, because they come from love—and *love can heal all things!*

<u>Words that *Reveal*</u>

The greeting *Namaste*, which translates loosely to *the God in me honors the God in you*, directs us to be a witness to, and acknowledge the truth of another's divinity. A worthy goal for all of us is to think and speak the truth—the Divine Godly Truth about ourselves and others. Our spoken word, propelled by our breath of life, is very powerful. It goes out from our lips, gathers energy that matches our motives and emotions, and returns to us magnified. It then becomes our experience. We empower ourselves and others when we speak Divine Spiritual Truth. The *Unity Prayer of Protection* is a wonderful example of words that reveal the Truth:

The **Light** of God surrounds me;

The **Love** of God enfolds me;

The **Power** of God protects me;

The **Presence** of God watches over me.

This reminds us wherever we are, God is.

If your life is on the track you want, wonderful! Keep thinking and speaking words of joy, praise, gratitude and love, and your good will continue to multiply! If your life is not going the way you want, be mindful of what you are thinking and saying to yourself and about others. Ascend to a higher truth and throw off negativity, focusing instead on what you have the power to change—such as your own thoughts, words and actions. Begin *now* to change the thought conditions that may precipitate, perpetuate, or feed negative experiences. Even if you have been victimized, overly identifying as a victim may only reinforce the negativity you survived. Own and declare your survivorship instead! We are *more* than our experiences.

You have the power to make positive changes, and to create a new future. It starts with the thoughts and words within you right now. Much of what you are experiencing today may be the consequence of what you thought or felt in the past. Choose kind words. Choose words that express the Godly Truth, especially about yourself. Choose words that *heal,* and *reveal* what you *do* want to experience. You will find that thought-by-thought, word-by-word, and day-by-day, your life, your joy, your health, and your good will improve and increase! So Be It.

AFFIRMATIONS

My words have the power to uplift and heal myself and others.

Today I use words that are kind and true, and my life improves.

Love is the Truth of my Being. I think, speak, and act from Love.

INTUITION: TRUSTING YOUR INNER VOICE

Life is full of situations that require a quick decision, reasoned discernment, or careful evaluation. Sometimes logic or reason reveals the answer, but what about the times we must call on our *intuition* for guidance? I'm reminded of the famous Yogi Berra quote, "If you come to a fork in the road, take it!"

How can we determine which inner voice to follow? The louder voice is usually based in ego or logic. The intuitive voice of spirit is usually subtle and quiet. Can I trust my answer and are there any guidelines that I can use?

Let's discuss how to discern more clearly the qualities, signs, and signals from the Higher Self, and how the ego can trick or distract us. We need the ego in order to function in the material world. However, the ego can become inflated and distort our perceptions, and even override our intuition. *How can we learn to contain or transcend the ego?*

It won't work to resist or try to outsmart it! If you engage the ego, it just fights harder, justifies its position, and gets stronger. One way to deal with the ego is simply to observe, notice its voice, and dismiss it. Say to yourself, *Oh...there goes my ego again, trying to create big drama.* Then just *let it go* without engaging it. Take a moment to get quiet and go within to Spirit.

I often ask myself, *What would a Master do? What would Love do in this situation?* I then remember that the spirit of love is within me, and I can draw on Infinite Intelligence to discern what's best to do. A good affirmation is: *Ego step aside; Spirit come forth!*

The ego can cause a lot of suffering, especially through judgment and criticism. When ego takes on the role of the Judge, it is often the loudest voice in our own head. It says ugly things like, *That was stupid,* or *You're not good enough, smart enough, not disciplined enough, you don't do enough—you're just not enough! You're not doing anything right!*

The loving Spirit within says, *You are my beloved, in whom I am well-pleased. You are worthy of all the good you can imagine. It is awaiting your acceptance. I love you just the way you are right now. We are One.* If the Judge starts shouting lies, take the power away from the lies and judgment by telling yourself the truth. Just observe, and then replace the lies with love. Listen to the voice of Spirit.

Let's look at some ways to tune in to the voice of love, strengthening it within ourselves. It is necessary to turn within and *connect consciously with your heart*. It is the center of light, love, and peace. There are many ways to tune into our higher thoughts and vibrations. One of my beloved teachers, the Rev. Wilma Arnott, reminds us simply to, "Think good thoughts, read good books, listen to good music, and speak good words."

People can connect to their hearts in many ways such as: deep breathing, meditation, focused movement, chanting, and music. Immersing ourselves in Nature also opens up our hearts. Keep it simple, and let it be easy. Bring an empty heart that Spirit can fill with light, love, and peace. *Be still and know that I Am God. All is One.*

Just as in any worthwhile relationship, it takes time and attention to cultivate your conscious connection with the God of your being, your Higher Self. It must become a habit to call on the power of your Godhood, to think with compassion and love, and to claim your spiritual authority in any situation.

If possible, take a few minutes at the beginning of each day to get quiet, listening to the voice of love and encouragement within. One builds spiritual muscle by communing with Spirit. It takes practice to call forth Spirit in any situation. A metaphysical classic by Emmet Fox entitled The Golden Key provides a powerful tool for success, "Instead of thinking about the difficulty, problem or challenge, *Think about God Instead."*

Another helpful technique to develop is called *Mindfulness,* or *Mindful Awareness.* The Buddhists teach this very well. This is so effective, because it keeps our full attention in the present moment. Mindfulness focuses on the eternal quality of Now; this is where miracles of peace, creativity, solutions, healing, and empowerment occur.

One can call forth the Infinite Intelligence of God right now, and apply it to any challenge or dilemma. Through our Higher Self, we perceive new possibilities and solutions; we sense the interconnectedness of all life. A feeling of gratitude, confidence, and peace fortifies us. We can imagine being healed; we can feel wholeness and strength. The ego loves to dwell in the past with blame and excuses, and to create fear about the future. Cultivating mindfulness helps keep the ego under control. Good self-care includes mindfulness.

When we purify our minds, bodies, and environments, we strengthen the filter of protection in this material world of pollution and static. We must keep the filter clean to be strong and balanced as we deal with this changing world.

When you receive a hunch, intuition, or message, ask yourself, *Am I supposed to pay attention to this message?* Ego may occasionally lead us into an unpleasant, possibly even dangerous situation in an attempt to please someone. We may occasionally ignore a subtle inner warning, or compromise our values to gain the attention, favor, or approval of someone. It is important to pay attention to the warning signals our bodies or inner voices are giving us in order to keep our boundaries strong.

Keeping yourself safe and healthy in the material world is your right and obligation. Remove yourself immediately in any appropriate manner from a threatening emotional or physical situation. The moment you are aware that you may be compromised, do not feel safe, or that your healthy boundaries have been breached, consciously call upon your Guardian Angel or any spiritual protector to guard and guide you. In your mind, you can ask a Being of Light to take charge of a dangerous or abusive person, and lead them away from you. You have the responsibility to honor your own divinity, and do what is necessary. Sometimes that means keeping a strong boundary by saying *No*, turning away, or even ending a relationship.

How can we really know whether our messages, hunches, or intuitions are from Spirit or Ego?

The following guidelines are quite simple:

How does your body feel?

If you feel peaceful and relaxed, it's probably Spirit. If you feel anxious, nervous or fearful, it's probably ego.

Am I in the present moment and mindful?

If yes, Spirit is guiding. If you're thinking about the past or future, it's probably ego. Spirit speaks with calm and quiet inner authority. Ego stirs up lots of noise, confusion, drama and fear.

Is this the voice of the inner critic, or the voice of love?

If my thoughts conjure fear, blame, or anxiety, then they are certainly coming from the ego. If they calm and relax me, filling me with compassion, hope and love, then the intuition or message is absolutely from Spirit.

Let's look at some characteristic differences between the Spirit and Ego:

Ego is very self-important, says *I, me,* and *mine*
Spirit exhibits generosity, is concerned with *you* and *yours*

Ego is often stuck in the past
Spirit lives in the present moment

Ego is selfish, insecure, feels disconnected
Spirit shares with others, is secure, promotes connection

Ego is fearful, feels lack and separation, expects the worst
Spirit trusts God's good, knows there's plenty, is optimistic

Ego is discontented, judges self and others
Spirit is joyful, kind, compassionate, accepts others

Ego often causes suffering
Spirit promotes healing

Ego often has a *know-it-all* attitude
Spirit has an intrinsic humility

Ego makes lots of excuses and blames others
Spirit takes personal responsibility, has natural authority

Ego loves to make everything complicated
Spirit keeps things simple

Ego is never satisfied, can't get *enough*
Spirit is content, satisfied, feels deep peace

Ego loves to create lots of drama
Spirit speaks quietly, clearly, and calmly

Ego wants to manipulate and change others
Spirit looks to inner power, is willing to change self

Ego criticizes and tears down others
Spirit encourages and praises others

Ego sometimes lies to protect itself
Spirit tells the truth, values integrity

Ego always wants to be *right*
Spirit wants to harmonize, listens to others

Ego takes everything personally, is easily
offended
Spirit is gracious, does not take offense

Ego makes the body feel anxious, nervous, tight
Spirit relaxes and opens up the body with
breath and peace

Ego is self-serving and fearful
Spirit is loving and serves others

—Ego or Spirit © 2014 Pamela Crofoot Desvernine

Remember, Spirit will be loving, peaceful, encouraging, and clear. It is *the still small voice within*. Spirit has the power to create something new and wonderful in the present moment—even miracles. **Listen. Love. Serve.** This is how Spirit works *for* you, and *through* you!

Do not curse the darkness. God needs each of us to radiate the Divine Light within, now more than ever. Trust and follow your inner Spirit. The voice of Divine Love will always and forever lead you to greater good!

AFFIRMATIONS

I am One with God. I recognize and trust the voice of Love.

I call forth my Higher Spirit; I command ego to step aside.

I let my Light shine in Peace, Power, Service, and Love.

HELLO WORLD!

A cherished teacher of mine, Rev. Dr. Orrin Moen, encouraged his students to affirm the, "Joyous expectancy of only Good." I use this daily to set a positive intention for harmonious interactions in the world. It sends the light of joy ahead as I tend to my tasks out in the *Big World*. Rarely do I return home without having had a special or even magical encounter. Another thought which paves a smoother path is to remember that we are divinely connected with *all* life. A light goes out from our hearts when we intentionally look for and see the spark of the Divine in those we encounter.

Years ago, my husband Des was at a crossroads in his life. He had finished two tours of duty with the U.S. Army and had recently graduated from Fordham University. Several business opportunities had come his way and he was also considering applying to the F.B.I. Some close family friends in Florida invited Des for a visit. It was there that he met an accomplished older gentleman whose wisdom and insights influenced the rest of Des' life.

This gentleman was the president of the Crucible Steel Corporation in Pittsburgh. While they relaxed on the deck overlooking a lovely lake, here's what the wise man told Des, "Our company hires a lot of good people with brilliant minds to design and engineer our products. These geniuses come from the best schools in the country, and we pay them well. However, the person who is most rare and hard to find in business is someone who has common sense, and can get along with people!" Subsequently, Des consciously cultivated his communication and people skills. Fortunately, he already had lots of common sense! These *rare* qualities served him well and earned him a great career and reputation in the F.B.I.

Des genuinely cared about people. He gained the respect and trust of his colleagues and even many of his criminal subjects—some of whom became informants. He supervised over 20 relocated witnesses, providing essential support to many of their families as they adjusted to a new life under government protection.

Albert Einstein gave us a clever puzzle to ponder, "Not everything that can be counted counts, and not everything that counts can be counted." Let's look at a few things that really count in successfully relating to people. A *smile* is the Universal Key to opening the door to positive interactions. A smile speaks every language in the world. Another quite obvious skill which is noticeably missing these days is making *eye contact.* My Uncle Howard was a master at making someone feel they were the most important person in the room. By looking at them with his kind eyes, listening attentively, and being 100% present in the moment, everyone felt his love. As a young man, he founded the House Ear Institute in 1946. His biography, For the World to Hear documents his dedication to enabling others to hear.

Another small but important habit is to remember the courtesy of saying, *Please* and *Thank You* often. Those who have worked with the public in any form of service quickly become aware of a customer's energy and attitude. With each interaction, whether by phone, electronic, or in person, we have the opportunity to set a pleasant tone for a positive connection. Today, most cashiers, servers, and customer support people wear name badges or say their names. When it's appropriate, using a person's name sends a message of respect, honors their individuality, and helps make an encounter more gracious and personal.

Des delighted in connecting with people by using their name, and asking where they grew up. He almost always found something in common with them. A couple of years ago, our goddaughter, Francis, fulfilled one of Des' life-long dreams—a road trip to Zion National Park and the Grand Canyon. After a morning ride, we decided to eat at Zion's Historic Lodge. We arrived just four minutes after they closed for brunch. Fortunately, a friendly young woman made an exception and brought us to a table on the scenic deck. In his genuinely caring grandfatherly manner, Des asked her name and where she was from. Ashley (also our granddaughter's name) was from North Carolina, and working at Zion for the summer to earn money for college. Des commented that N.C. was his favorite state. We had many friends there, including his F.B.I partner. Tearfully, Ashley confided in us that she was very homesick. Just reminiscing with us about her home state had lifted her spirits. The connection we made from simply asking her name and caring about her story resulted in a warm and memorable experience for all of us. We were stunned when the manager came to our table later and told us that Ashley had bought our brunch because we "felt like family!"

If a person is a little grumpy or unresponsive to an attempt to connect, don't take it personally. Give them an *extra* smile, kind words, and a silent blessing. We'll never know if they were up all night with a sick child or parent. They may be in pain, grief, or working a double shift to cover someone else. Take every opportunity to be the light and compassion of God. Your smile and blessing become substance for the Angels to use in helping people.

The following excerpt from the *"Paradoxical Commandments"* by Dr. Kent Keith reminds us to give people the benefit of the doubt and take the spiritual high road of kindness and tolerance

People are often illogical, unreasonable, and
self-centered.
Love them anyway.
The good you do today will be forgotten
tomorrow.
Do good anyway.
Honesty and frankness make you vulnerable.
Be honest and frank anyway.

Everyone is at a different point on their journey of life. Shine your own light, and recognize theirs.

When we engage with the world, it's inevitable that we may occasionally find ourselves in an unpleasant or even unjust situation. We may also have to deal with difficult people. Misunderstandings, injustices, and serious differences happen within families, among friends, and in the larger society. We aspire to find some common ground, and a place to resolve conflict. This wise thought from Rumi, a 13th century Persian poet guides us, "Out beyond the ideas of wrongdoing and rightdoing there is a field. I'll meet you there." How can we address differences with thoughtful consideration and respect?

I'd like to share a couple of approaches that help me remain honest with myself, speak my truth, and maintain my peace and integrity. I intentionally prepare for peace. Rather than react or feed conflict, I immediately choose peace. This has taken a lot of practice, but it comes naturally now. It's all about clear and respectful communication with the intention of building a bridge and not a wall. Remember, it's never about changing someone else. Try to find something to agree on; this helps set the tone for further discussion, reconciliation, and resolution. Sometimes I must set my ego aside, or summon the humility to apologize. It's up to me to be clear, strong, and do no harm, especially with words or a decision that I may regret later.

Occasionally, we all face situations that despite our best efforts remain unresolved. In that case I ask myself, *What would a Spiritual Master say or do in this situation?* Simply asking this question reminds me to pause and listen for guidance. Sometimes I am impressed to wait to allow confusion or inharmonious energies to settle; perhaps a little time is needed for more clarity. Sometimes the guidance is immediate and strong for a new approach towards resolution. Even if a situation remains unresolved, aligning with a Spiritual Master helps me remain patient, positive, and peaceful.

Every day I aspire to live my higher values of peace, harmony and integrity. Therefore, I must continually cultivate understanding, compassion, and be aware of my motives. Humility is required to create resolutions, especially if forgiveness or compromise is in order. My wise Mom affirmed that she was *willing to be willing* to make necessary changes in her thinking or actions. What, or who, do I need to release in order to restore my inner peace? Pain tends to live at the point of resistance—*what we resist persists*. I also affirm that I am willing to let go of anything within me that blocks my joy of living. Rev. Dr. Arlene Bump had a humorous and insightful perspective, "Everyone blesses us—some by coming, and some by leaving."

The peace we cultivate in ourselves contributes to more peace in the world. By dissolving barriers, we can relate to each other as one family in God. With trust and discernment, we step into our worldly encounters and activities with confidence. The more we perceive the Unity of all life; feelings of separation and *otherness* are replaced by compassion, connection and interdependence. As we each bring our inner light, love, and peace to our interactions, we make this a friendlier, more peaceful world. Remember we're all in this thing called Life *together*!

AFFIRMATIONS

I intentionally prepare for harmonious encounters with people.

My communications are clear, caring, and life-affirming.

I feel at ease and connected in the world because I am guided by Divine Love.

MASTERING PEACE

L ife is often challenging. Worry and stress impact our sleep, eating, and overall health. In the material world there are obvious reasons for concern which can lead to mass fear and despair. However, if we succumb to the way of the world, we actually contribute to the problems and darkness. Negativity and despair are disempowering. We must use our spiritual lens to see the world differently in order to restore our personal balance, be a positive influence, and cultivate peace of mind.

Jesus the Christ demonstrated mastery over the material world, and showed us the power to invoke peace and calm over the stormy winds and sea. We too can develop mastery over the material world and our own stormy emotional seas. As we build a reservoir of inner peace, the world is less disturbing, and we *become* the peace we want to feel and see.

Spiritual Masters understand and use the Higher Laws. They have learned to discipline their senses and focus their minds. They observe the material world with compassion, maintaining emotional poise and mental balance. They serve in love and act with discernment, using their talents to heal and uplift whomever and whatever comes across their path of experience. They consciously align with the Infinite, with God, through mindfulness, meditation and prayer, and seem unperturbed by the chaos of the world. Dr. Ernest Holmes describes *peace* as, "A state of inner calm so complete that nothing can disturb it."

Many of us practice mindfulness and compassion, but have you ever thought you could actually *become* a master of the spiritual and material worlds? Does that sound egotistical to you? Does that seem like too high a goal? Well, I have news for you: it is not only possible, it is a divine assignment you are being called to do—yes you! I believe that you are incarnated at this time for a divine purpose. God needs you to express your innate divinity and light, here and now.

To become more masterful in your life, please consider the following suggestions:

Put God First

"Seek ye first the Kingdom of Heaven and all else will be added." Matthew 6.33.

Affirm that *I am in God, God is in me, and We are One*. No cry for help for yourself or another ever goes in vain. Many people desperately turn to prayer as a last resort. Let us remember to go into prayer as our *first* response to a need. Choose to put your trust and faith in the goodness and Infinite Intelligence of our Loving Creator God. It is one sure way to feel more peace.

Learn To Control Your Mind

There are many effective methods which can be used to gain mastery over our thoughts and minds. Spiritual disciplines such as meditation, prayer, and movement such as yoga, provide the quietness needed to be receptive to our intuition and spiritual guidance. When setting intentions and goals, your mind is a powerful ally. Consciously use your imagination to *visualize* and get the *feeling* of what you want. You create the life and experiences you desire through the power of your mind. Remember, the sweetest desires of your heart and the loftiest dreams of your soul were planted there by the Great Spirit. When you focus your thoughts and master your mind, you can truly turn your dreams into reality!

We are happiest when we feel balanced and peaceful. The amazing thing is that by cultivating inner peace, it becomes a source of strength, of confidence, even an attitude with which we can successfully meet life's challenges and experiences. Therefore, if something happens to knock us off-balance, it's just temporary. We use spiritual practices to get our higher perspective back quickly and return to love, balance, and peace. Let's look at some of those spiritual practices.

Be Still: Stop and Breathe

People often respond to stress by unconsciously holding their breath, causing irregular and shallow breathing. This creates more anxiety and depletes oxygen which then interferes with clear thinking. Take some slow deep breaths to relax the body and clear the mind. Consciously claim your spiritual power over a material situation. Use affirmations to get back on track and regain your equilibrium:

I call forth God's Intelligence, Power, Wisdom,
and Compassion in me now!
God is in this experience. I am not alone.
I expect the best outcome.
I ask God within to show me the best way now.

Be Present in the Moment

Most of our anxieties come when we regret the past or fear the future. As Louise Hay reminds us, "The Point of Power is in the Present Moment." What am I doing this moment to build the life I desire?

Trust and Surrender to God's Love and Goodness

Ernest Holmes states, "There is a Power greater than I am that I can use." This power is a combination of Divine Intelligence and love. It comes through your own mind and heart. It is for you and not against you. God's will is for your highest good and greatest joy. Trust that you are being guided and directed by this Divine Intelligence. Say to yourself:

The mind I am using is the Mind of God within me.
Everything I need to know, do, or stop doing, is
revealed to me harmoniously.
I quiet my mind and listen.
I trust the Divine Flow of God's Good for me now.
I release all fear and anxiety, knowing that God
is working everything out for my Good.

Forgive

Forgiveness is a tender and sometimes difficult subject. Almost everyone carries mental, emotional, or physical wounds of greater or lesser degrees. It is a natural response to close our hearts against the perpetrators, often harboring anger, resentment, or even obsessive hatred. Those thoughts and emotions become blockages in our hearts, constricting the flow of our true nature, which is love. Extending forgiveness does not mean that we condone or approve of the offense, abuse, or injurious circumstance. There may be times when it is necessary to enforce accountability, which requires courage and fortitude. Forgiveness means that we now love and empower ourselves to do whatever is needed to set ourselves free—and create a new future.

Maya Angelou suggests that loving oneself is necessary *"for-giving-up"* the bondage of our inner pain, and the constraints of the past. We can open ourselves to the love which brings healing and closure to the wound, even if scarring remains. A mental, emotional or physical scar is proof of healing, an acknowledgement that we survived the trauma. We are now liberated to reframe our self-identity. The time and energy we once spent in anger, hatred or pain is freed up to give more love to ourselves, others, and our future.

Practice forgiving, reframing, and releasing anything that impedes love. God supplies enough love to heal whatever needs forgiveness. Set yourself free to heal and look forward to greater peace. Kahlil Gibran provides a unique perspective in <u>The Prophet</u>, "The deeper that sorrow carves into your being, the more joy you can contain."

Expect the Best

Do your part, do your best, and look for the best in others. Be kind, patient, and tolerant. Let go of drama and claim grace and ease in your circumstances. Remember, with God there's always a way, always an answer. You are becoming a Master of the material world. Watch with gratitude and amazement how the Infinite Intelligence and Goodness of God is revealed in your life. God needs *you* to be the peace in your world, and that in turn magnifies the peace in the outer world. Choose to call forth the peace of God within that nothing can disturb!

AFFIRMATIONS

Regardless of appearances, God is turning everything to Good.

I am willing to release all blockages to Love.

God's peace fills me now and radiates into the world.

HEART OF THE MATTER

Physically, the heart is an organ that keeps us alive through a coordinated network of cells beating together. Spiritually, the heart is the center of love, the force that makes our lives worthwhile. Globally, the heart is a symbol of a new organizing principle for how to live together on this finite jewel of a planet.

—Anodea Judith

A human being is a wondrous and complex creation originating within the Infinite Intelligence and Love of God. The essential pulse of life in our bodies emanates from the physical heart. The heart is arguably our most sensitive organ, immediately responding to our internal and external environments. Most people have experienced the thrill of falling in love. Many of us know the pain of a broken heart from loss, grief, or rejection. Nearly all people know the joy of love for family, friends, and pets. Some have experienced the ecstasy of spiritual love for God or an ideal. The body registers every thought and feeling of love. Regardless of the type or degree of love, it is beneficial to the body and soul.

The spiritualized heart develops as our consciousness expands, melding the brain, mind, and heart. We begin to literally *think* through our hearts. We've all had plenty of examples in our lives when our logical brain had a plan; but our heart intervened, overrode the logic and made a *new* choice from love. Although we appreciate and respect the brain, let's consider living more connected to the intelligence and motives of the heart.

I have never heard of anyone in this School of Earth Life who has escaped physical, mental, emotional, or spiritual challenges. Love has the power to transform, heal or transmute any negative experience, condition, or relationship. We have the power and spiritual authority to direct and apply that love. As we claim our own power to transform any experience, through love, we gain access to the infinite possibilities of the Great Creator.

Our source of life and love is God. "God is love, and

those who live in love, live in God, and God lives in them." 1 John 4.16. Just as we cannot separate the wave from the ocean, we cannot be separated from God. Mary Baker Eddy, founder of Christian Science, put it this way, "Divine Love has met and always will meet every human need." When we acknowledge, prioritize, and cultivate the qualities of God within ourselves, *especially love,* we can expect our lives to improve, and we'll experience more joy, grace, and peace.

The Master Christ Jesus gave us what is known as the Great Commandment. It says that we are to love God with all our heart, soul, strength and mind, and love our neighbor as ourselves. Some people are concerned that if they put God first in their lives, they will have to give up a lot. However, it is my experience that as I consciously align with my inner divinity and love myself more, my attractions to unhealthy or destructive impulses or habits fade. I am no longer fighting myself because my urges and desires have changed at a deep inner level.

Putting God first is not about sacrifice or deprivation. As Ernest Holmes reminds us, "The Will of God is always towards that which expresses more life and happiness." We build our own healthy self-esteem by developing our relationship with our inner God. As we learn to love and value ourselves more, our capacity to love others expands. Let's look at what can bring more *heart*, that is more *love*, to ourselves, our relationships, and the matters we deal with in life.

Almost everyone I know has struggled with low self-esteem and doubt at some time in their lives. Society broadcasts many false, detrimental messages. Most harmful messaging starts in childhood. Children are often given critical and mean messages saying they are wrong, bad, or not good enough. These can come from misguided parents, teachers, other children, and media rhetoric. With enough repetitions, children may start to believe these negative messages. The tragic result is the current epidemic of childhood bullying, and the alarming statistics of depression and subsequent suicides in all age groups.

Although this is a complex issue, here are some thoughts to consider. One of the most effective ways to heal the wounds of low self-esteem, no matter the origin, is to stop comparing oneself to others. Stop accepting the criticism of others and the false messages you may have believed in the past. Be on the alert for negative messages. Consciously decide to turn to the spiritual truth of yourself; you are a unique and precious being of light, you were created from the Divine seed of Love. You have unique talents to express; you have a unique purpose to fulfill. You are loved, lovable, and loving! Libby Roderick wrote a beautiful song that continues to touch me deeply whenever it comes to mind:

How could anyone ever tell you
You were anything less than beautiful?
How could anyone ever tell you
You were less than whole?
How could anyone fail to notice
That your loving is a miracle?
How deeply you're connected to my soul.

—How Could Anyone? © Libby Roderick Music 1988

When you free yourself from the bondage of low self-esteem and criticism, you approve, nurture, and love yourself. The appreciation, understanding, and compassion you give to yourself, you can now extend to others. Rumi poetically stated, "Your task is not to seek for love, but merely to seek all the barriers within yourself that you have built against it."

We are never separated from the love of God. The figurative arms of the Divine Father/Mother God are always welcoming us back to our true home of love and peace in the heart. The following line by comedienne Lily Tomlin always makes me laugh, "I always wanted to be somebody, but now I see that I should have been more specific." The truth is that you *are* somebody—somebody special and worthy of your own approval and love! Your identity is clear and secure; you are a beloved child of God, a complete original. Stay true to yourself. Cultivate, appreciate, and enjoy your uniqueness. The philosopher Nietzsche wrote, "And those who danced were thought to be insane by those who could not hear the music." Keep dancing to your own inner music! Stop comparing yourself to others. Judy Garland advised that it's better to be a first-rate version of yourself than a second-rate version of somebody else.

On the firm foundation of God's Love and our healthy self-esteem, we can build authentic and fulfilling relationships with others. It is often said that we learn the most from those we live with. It's certainly true for me! I was blessed to grow up with parents and step-parents who were loving, encouraging, and wise. As a family we cultivated spiritual strength. The uplifting and inspiring spiritual materials our Mom read to us after dinner each night had lasting value. No family is exempt from crises, challenges, or tragedies, and ours was no exception. But love, mutual support, faith and prayer guided us through many challenges, including divorce, extreme physical illness, and the sudden death of my brother at age 26 in an automobile accident. Along my path, through observation, study, and experience, I have learned a few things I'd like to share which contribute to healthy relationships and a meaningful, harmonious life.

One of the values our family lived by is, *different isn't wrong*. Many parents think that being *fair* with their children means having uniform rules and rewards. This usually backfires, due to the uniqueness and age of each child. If parents cannot be consistent in applying these rules, a child may perceive unfairness, and resentments can build up in the family. Although unfairness may be a fact of life, no one wants to foster a victim mentality in their child. A healthy family dynamic encourages cooperation and respect rather than jealousy and mean competition. Fairness doesn't mean uniformity or even equality. My brother, sister and I had very different personalities, interests and talents. As younger children, each of us handled responsibility differently and earned different privileges. The rules that applied to one didn't necessarily apply to the other two. We were always urged to honor our differences, and not be jealous of them. These values contributed to our own self-esteem, and became part of our natural perspective on the world.

It has been my experience that most damage to intimate relationships, family ties, and friendships stem from misunderstandings, mean-spirited words and actions, and/or intentional ill-will. The emotional harm and psychological wounds from words spoken in anger or with intentional harm can last a lifetime. As I've mentioned previously, your breath of life and choice of words, backed by feelings, are more powerful than you can imagine. Like a boomerang, they gather resonant energy and can return to you with even greater impact or consequences. We all value honesty and telling our truth. Sometimes a communication requires us to be frank and clear. We may even have to deliver difficult or unpleasant news, which takes tact and courage. I believe that honesty needs to include respect and kindness. Being honest *never* justifies a cruel, demeaning, or brutal communication. Learning to express yourself clearly and respectfully even under stress, creates an atmosphere of integrity, trust, and confidence. Ultimately, nothing but good comes when you use words that encourage, are kind, respectful, honest, and loving.

At least 50% of effective communication is *listening*. In his book, <u>Mindfulness</u>, the Buddhist Monk Thich Nhat Hahn says, "To listen is to love." Attentive listening is a way to bring our heart and respect to any verbal communication. If or when we interrupt someone, we're giving the speaker the message that their expression, thoughts, or feelings are not as important as our own. Listen to understand.

The value of listening is illustrated in the following conversation that Steven Spielberg had in an interview with James Lipton, founder of the Actors Studio in New York. At the end of every show, Mr. Lipton asked each guest the same question, "If Heaven exists, what would you like to hear God say when you arrive at the Pearly Gates?" Without hesitating, Spielberg responded, "Thanks for listening." It's evident from his successes that Steven listens a lot!

We are occasionally tempted to think that we know what's best for someone else. We think their problem would be solved if they'd just *listen to me and do it my way*. We can't change anyone else. We can't possibly know what's really best for another, or understand what their soul's purpose or lessons are in this lifetime. We can, however, change our own perceptions and attitudes towards someone's choices and behaviors. By holding them in prayer and sending Divine Love, we empower the best in them. This helps us release them to their greater good without judgment. Remember, God's love and care enfolds all of us unconditionally, whether we are able to acknowledge this or not.

Humor is one of the most effective tools to diffuse a tense situation and restore harmony. I'm lucky that both my husband Des and goddaughter Francis are half-Irish and very, very funny. Laughter often comes to the rescue, averting a potential problem. One time, Des was having some mild digestion issues. I was certain from my observations that it was because he was taking big bites of food and swallowing without much chewing. One week I started reminding him at nearly every meal to take smaller bites and chew more. A couple of days later he'd had enough of my *reminders*. As his frustration and agitation grew, he exclaimed, "I chew! I *Chew*! I CHEW!" I responded with, "Gesundheit!" We both burst out laughing. By the way—I stopped my nagging.

One summer, Francis and I attended a Family Reunion in central Indiana. The reunion venue was about an hour from our hotel through beautiful, identical, endless, acres of corn and soy bean fields. On our way back to the hotel, I was grateful for the GPS on my phone and for Francis as navigator. To visitors like us, the road names in farm country are very confusing, like S. 900 E., or W. 375 N. Evidently, one can be on the right road—in the wrong county! Francis and I were tired and knew that we and the GPS were *lost*. As the sun sank, frustration and tension grew between us, but Francis came up with a brilliant idea, "Let's just pull over and make each other *laugh*!" That alone broke the tension; we pulled over, laughed, calmed down, and reset the GPS destination. We soon found the Interstate that zipped us back to the hotel in time for a late supper. Whew! Finding the humor in almost any tense situation can de-escalate it. Laughter in our day brings back balance, harmony, and fun.

Friendships enhance the quality and enjoyment of life. Des was a true master in the *Art of Friendship*. His extraordinary ability to engage and immediately connect with new people was natural and a delight to witness. He and Kermit the Frog had the same dilemma, "There's no word yet for old friends who've just met." The breadth and depth of his friendships were particularly evident in the last 6 months of his 89 years. Many international and local friends made special trips to visit and enjoy him in home hospice. He had touched their hearts with his genuine caring, and many told us that Des was their best friend. How could this be? It was because he knew how to *be* a friend. Des made people laugh, but he also knew how to listen with his heart. If someone came to his mind, he'd spontaneously pick up the phone or send an email to say he was just thinking of them. He kept Francis and me busy tracking down people whose contact information had changed. Our skills as Private Investigators came in handy! Everyone felt better after a conversation with Des.

Many people may be on the shy side, or have just a few friends. Friendship is not a numbers game. A person's value does not depend on how many friends one has—it's quality over quantity. Nurture your connections of the heart in any creative way you can. Kahlil Gibran expresses it beautifully in The Prophet, "And in the sweetness of friendship let there be laughter and sharing of pleasures. For in the dew of little things the heart finds its morning and is refreshed."

I believe that Creator God is the initial giver of life, including my life and yours. We are the receivers. Life is made up of countless circles of giving and receiving. A healthy circle is manifested when we express our own divinity. We reflect back to God our appreciation of life by unfolding our unique qualities and giving love and service to others. Every aspect of life depends on circulation, ebb and flow, in and out, gather and release. Most of our troubles can be traced to blockages in circulation. This can be seen in our bodies, but also applies to our finances, communications, and relationships. As we learn to balance giving and receiving, we keep the life force clear and flowing. We open to receive the constant supply of God's unlimited good for us, and send it back out into the world as light, love, and service. The Divine Circle is free-flowing and complete through us.

There is a Universal Principle which operates in life: *Whatever we dwell on increases.* It works whether we give attention to life-enhancing thoughts and actions, or to detrimental, limiting ideas and behaviors. This Principle is impartial, and will magnify whatever positive or negative energies we give it. Here's a guide by Oscar Wilde, "The difference between an Optimist and Pessimist is droll; the Optimist sees the donut, and the Pessimist see the hole!" As we stay tuned to the Source with our faith and gratitude, we enjoy the abundant flow of good and supply.

There was a time long ago when I had gotten temporarily out of alignment with God. I was critical, judgmental, very unhappy with myself and life, and was dwelling on   feelings of lack. I kept saying to myself, "Something's gotta give!" Finally, the realization came that it was *I* who had to give. I had to *give up* my resentments, unforgivingness, and low self-esteem which were blocking the circulation of my happiness and supply. I started consciously practicing gratitude for my health, job, and all the blessings in my life. As a tangible symbol, I decided to give a gift back to God. Although my finances still needed some healing, I was very healthy physically. The gift I could give was to donate a pint of my blood. This precious life force given freely to me could be passed to someone in need. This act reinforced in my own mind that the circle of giving and receiving was sacred and never-ending.

Let's look at the circulation of thoughts and ideas. We've often heard that what we send out consistently in thought, word, and action returns to us multiplied. If you feel lack in any area of your life, stop dwelling on what you perceive is missing. Instead, give constant attention to what you *do* want to experience or manifest. Use your affirmative thoughts, words and actions to positively support your heart's desires. The Infinite Creator is not withholding anything from you. Your words of gratitude, praise and love become the foundation of a joyful life.

You'll find that your blessings come faster than the candy on the factory assembly line with Lucy and Ethel!

All of Creation is the out-picturing of God's Divine Love. The seed of Divine Love is born into every soul. We relate to others with love, because we behold the God in them. Humanity has not fully grasped that we are completely interconnected and interdependent with *all* forms of life. We are literally *One in and with* all dimensions of the Universe.

There's a cute story of a Sunday School class of 4-year-olds who spent the hour drawing pictures. Before cleaning up, the teacher went around the table asking each child about their drawing. Rosie was eager to share, saying proudly, "It's a picture of God." When the teacher mentioned that no one knew what God looked like, Rosie declared confidently, "They will now!" With every kind word, action, and gesture of love, *you* are showing the world what God looks like.

The beloved Fred Rogers inspires us to embody God's Love in the following passage, "At the center of the Universe is a loving heart that continues to beat and that wants the best for every person. Anything we can do to help foster the intellect and spirit and emotional growth of our fellow human beings; this is our job. Those of us who have this particular vision must continue against all odds." As God's Ambassadors we work diligently to express love through service thereby bringing Heaven to Earth.

Ernest Holmes reminds us, "Love is the Cosmic Force whose sweep is irresistible." Nothing can resist Divine Love. With God all things are possible. With love, anything and everything is created, resolved, dissolved, changed, or healed, revealing our Divine Wholeness. Let us open our hearts to allow even more love to flow in and out. The *Heart of the Matter* is expressed beautifully in 1 Corinthians 13.13, "And now these three remain: faith, hope, and love. **But the greatest of these is love.**"

AFFIRMATIONS
I am Loved, Lovable, and Loving.
I see the world through the eyes of my heart.
I bring Love to all I say and do.

NEVER BEFORE

Never before has Humanity
    had such potential
    to fulfill the Divine Promise of Good.

Never before has the dawn of a new day
    been so precious.

Never before have personal and global choices
    had such tangible consequences.

Never before has Humanity
    been so powerful to perpetrate
    its own demise—
And take Nature with it.

Never before has it been so necessary for me
    to call forth the Highest Within;
    to take responsibility for my thoughts;
    to act in compassion and courage;
    to contribute constantly, in subtle and overt
    ways,
    to the Forces of Light;
And to remember,
I Am One with the Source of All.

—Never Before © *Pamela Desvernine 2014*

FURTHER READING

The books listed below contributed significantly to my spiritual growth, and continue to inspire and sustain me. I keep them within easy reach.

Gendler, J. Ruth. *The Book of Qualities.* Berkeley, CA: Turquoise Mountain Publications, 1984.

Hay, Louise. *Heal Your Body.* Carlsbad, CA: Hay House, Inc., 1982.

Hodson, Geoffrey. *The Kingdom of the Gods.* Adyar Madras 20, India: The Theosophical Publishing House, 1980.

Hicks, Esther and Jerry. *Ask and It Is Given: Learning to Manifest Your Desires* (The teachings of Abraham). Carlsbad, CA: Hay House, Inc., 2004.

Holmes, Ernest. *The Science of Mind.* New York: Dodd, Mead, & Company, 1938.

Kupferle, Mary L. *God Will See You Through.* Unity Village, MO: Unity School of Christianity, 1983.

Reid, John Stuart www.cymascope.com. 2021.

Spalding, Baird T. *Life and Teachings of the Masters of the Far East (Vol 1-5).* Los Angeles, CA: De Vorss & Co., 1924.

Three Initiates. *The Kybalion: Hermetic Philosophy.* Chicago, IL: The Yogi Publication Society, 1912.

Walker, DaEl The Crystal Awareness Institute. www.crystalawareness.com.

White Eagle. *Jesus, Teacher and Healer.* Hampshire, England: The White Eagle Publishing Trust, 1985.

Wilde, Stuart. *The Force.* Carlsbad, CA: Hay House, Inc., 1984

ABOUT THE AUTHOR

Pamela Crofoot Desvernine has devoted her life to God, Spirit, and service to others. Ms. Desvernine was the Board President of the Interfaith Celebration of Light Church in San Francisco for 16 years. She also contributed there as the pianist, frequent Sunday Speaker, Spiritual Healer, and Certified Medium.

In the early 1970s, she successfully helped launch and manage several renowned fine-dining restaurants throughout California, at a time when female managers in this field were rare.

In 1985, Pamela joined Desvernine Associates Inc., a Private Investigations and Security firm founded by her husband Graham "Des" Desvernine, a retired Special

Agent of the FBI—renowned for his premier undercover roles. She was Partner and Chief Operating Officer for over 30 years.

Since retiring, she serves on the Board of the Golden Gate Collectors, a non-profit organization which studies and supports the Fine Arts.

Her beloved husband Des crossed into the Higher Life in 2018. She lives in San Francisco, California, with her goddaughter Francis. Pamela loves music, laughing, praying, writing, drawing flowers, daily talks with her sister Debra, connecting with friends, and taking walks in nature.

MEMORIAL TRIBUTE

In Loving Memory of Graham "Des" Desvernine
aka *Mr. Wonderful*

Seeing death as the end of life
Is like seeing the horizon
as the end of the ocean.

—Ken Searles

My beloved husband Des passed to the Higher Life during the writing of this book. Since his passing, I rely on my spiritual foundation even more as I grieve, grow, and adjust to a new chapter in my life. My goddaughter Francis and I had the privilege of caring for him at home with the help of our extraordinary hospice team. We were especially blessed that Des had very little pain, and maintained his great personality and sense of humor. One day a hospice nurse asked him, "So Des, do you have any fears or anxiety about dying?" He cheerfully replied, "Oh no! I just look at death as the next great adventure!" Each day we endeavored to make his journey toward the Other Side meaningful, peaceful, and even joyful. The tools I share in this book helped all of us through that challenging time, allowing us to have the spiritual understanding to treasure every moment of this inevitable, sacred experience.

My life took a new direction the night I met Des in the early 1970s. Friends from Los Angeles arranged to visit me at the new restaurant I managed near the San Francisco Airport. They informed me that an old friend of theirs named Des, an F.B.I. Agent, would be joining us. Des was fascinating! As the evening progressed, Des revealed that he was working on four different undercover cases requiring four different aliases; one being a Mafia Don named Vic Rossi. That's why I started calling him *Mr. Wonderful* so I would not mess up his aliases!

Des also related that he was helping several relocated witnesses and their families who were in the Witness Protection Program, under the care of the U. S.

Government. The courageous testimonies of these people against deadly criminals caused their families to face extreme circumstances. Des was a steady and compassionate support in their difficult lives. I remember thinking at the time how amazing it was that with all he had seen and done during a lifetime in law enforcement, he was neither jaded nor cynical. In fact, he was the opposite. I discovered he had a very optimistic and compassionate outlook on life. He was humorous, generous, and had *kind* eyes despite having seen the worst of humanity's behavior in his line of work. As our relationship progressed, I knew Des was serious when he gave up his Sunday morning golf matches to join me at church! Mr. Wonderful and I were married a couple years later and some of my friends heard his true name for the first time during our wedding ceremony!

Des retired from the F.B.I. in 1980, after a legendary career. He was then recruited by the Marin County Sheriff's Department to apprehend a serial murderer: *The Trailside Killer*. The expertise he and his partner brought to the case resulted in a successful arrest and conviction.

Des then established Desvernine Associates Inc., a private investigations and security firm. As his business grew, he needed administrative help. I joined him as partner and C.O.O., working by his side for the next thirty years. Our lives were enriched by meaningful work, interesting travel, great employees and colleagues, and lots of laughter. Our mutual admiration, respect, trust, and deep love made it all possible.

Family was important to Des. He had three children by his first wife. As they all married, the family grew by six grandchildren. Des maintained strong and loving communications with them right up to his passing.

Des believed in giving back to the many organizations he supported and enjoyed. A passionate golfer, he volunteered for 26 years marshalling at the famed AT&T Golf Pro-Am in Pebble Beach, eventually serving there as Course Captain for many years. Professionally, Des served on the Board of Directors for the World Investigators Network. He also demonstrated his gratitude to God and Spirit by serving our church for sixteen years as an usher, speaker, and Board Member.

Des always enthusiastically supported me and my activities. His love, affection and care provided an environment of encouragement that helped me to blossom and fulfill my own potential. Since his passing, our love and relationship continues to evolve. A new language is developing between us. His many creative and humorous signs, symbols, and spirit communications show me daily that life and love go on. This quote by J.C. Jaynes brings great comfort as I grieve, "Memories are God's way of allowing us to hold on while letting go." With my whole heart I thank my beloved *Mr. Wonderful* for all he *continues* to be, and for his countless contributions to helping me unfold my highest potential. I am eternally blessed.

LOVE is FOREVER

Made in United States
North Haven, CT
04 August 2022

22269179R00071